Original title:
Cozy Fires, Christmas Choirs

Copyright © 2024 Creative Arts Management OÜ
All rights reserved.

Author: Zachary Prescott
ISBN HARDBACK: 978-9916-90-934-8
ISBN PAPERBACK: 978-9916-90-935-5

Warmth in the Winter Night

Snowflakes dance with gentle grace,
While hot cocoa warms my face.
I put on socks that don't quite match,
And laugh at my own sock attack.

The cat's curled up, a furry ball,
Stealing heat, stealing it all.
If only she could pay the bill,
I'd let her snooze—no need to chill!

Harmonies Beneath the Stars

Under stars, we sing our tune,
A chorus mixed with goofy swoon.
The dog howls back, he thinks he's nice,
As we try to hit that high note thrice.

Neighbors peek from curtains tight,
Wondering what's causing this fright.
A symphony of giggles and barks,
Our backyard feels like a park of quirks.

Flickering Lights and Gentle Songs

The lights flicker with a silly dance,
Like they're caught in winter's trance.
I sing off-key, my cat just stares,
At my lack of musical cares.

A ghostly voice from the TV plays,
Reminds me of my younger days.
As snacks pile high, the couch sinks low,
I smile at the warmth of the glow.

The Hearth's Embrace

The fire crackles, a warm delight,
As marshmallows roast, oh what a sight!
But one slipped down and fell on the floor,
Now the dog's gotten it—who needs more?

With blankets piled up to my chin,
I settle in for this cozy win.
The warmth wraps tight like a bear hug,
Yet somehow I still feel a little smug.

Lullabies of Winter

Snowflakes tumble, soft and light,
The penguins dance, oh what a sight!
Hot cocoa dreams in a snowy haze,
While squirrels scheme in winter's maze.

Chilly winds play in the trees,
As snowmen chat with playful ease.
The frost nips noses, cheeks so bright,
While winter wraps us in its white.

The Gathering's Melody

Gather 'round, it's feast time now,
Turkey gobbles, take a bow!
Pumpkin pie takes the stage so grand,
While chairs creak—a band so planned.

Cranberry sauce, a funky groove,
Dance 'round the table, it's time to move!
Auntie's jigs in her wild old shoes,
While Uncle Joe sings off-key blues.

Serene Shadows and Tender Songs

Under the stars, shadows play,
While crickets chirp the night away.
Fireflies glow like tiny dreams,
In the serenade, laughter beams.

Whispers of love in the cool night air,
With blankets wrapped, we haven't a care.
Songs of the heart, soft and sweet,
As moonlight dances, our souls meet.

Frosty Evenings and Soft Harmonies

Frosty evenings, hot tea cheers,
As we share giggles, spiced with fears!
The cat steals warmth upon my lap,
While the dog dreams of a frosty trap.

Blankets piled like snowy hills,
As laughter bubbles, oh what thrills!
With tales of ghosts that make us squirm,
We huddle close, safe from the term.

Nights Wrapped in Tender Notes

Under stars, we sway and twirl,
Laughter dances, a joyful whirl.
Songs of crickets fill the air,
As moonlight kisses our tousled hair.

A marshmallow roast gone slightly wrong,
We sing off-key, but still feel strong.
With blankets piled in cozy heaps,
We whisper secrets, while the world sleeps.

The Spirit of Togetherness

In a kitchen, chaos reigns supreme,
Flour on noses, it's a baking dream.
Eggs cracked with joy, sprinkles galore,
We laugh 'til we cry, who could ask for more?

Games of charades with questionable skill,
Dancing like penguins, we're never still.
Pizza's on fire, but spirits are high,
Together we cheer, 'let's just give it a try!'

Winter's Lullaby by Candlelight

Candlelight flickers, shadows play,
Hot cocoa spills, but that's okay.
With blankets wrapped, we warm our toes,
A snowman made of coffee woes.

Outside it snows, a fluffy mess,
While inside we wear our cozy dress.
Snowball fights with fierce delight,
We dive in drifts, oh what a sight!

Rustic Rhythms and Glowing Hearts

On porches swing our laughter bright,
With homemade jams and stars at night.
Fiddles play an old-time tune,
While fireflies dance under the moon.

A pie contest ends in sweet defeat,
Cherry juice stains from head to feet.
We raise our glasses, a clumsy cheer,
'To rustic rhythms and friends so dear!'

Laughter in the Glow

In the glow of the fridge's bright light,
Midnight snacks make the world feel right.
A cookie rolled off my sleepy face,
It wins the battle of this snack race.

The cat joins in, eyes wide with cheer,
Stealing my chips, oh dear, oh dear!
Crisps crunch like secrets shared at night,
We giggle together till dawn's first light.

Dividends of Delight

Investing in laughs, I check my book,
Each chuckle a dividend I gladly took.
Stocks in silliness rising and bright,
I sell my frowns, switching to delight.

Jokes on the wall, they're quite the asset,
My portfolio's humor? You can't assess it!
Market of giggles, watch the prices soar,
Laughter's a currency, worth much more.

Fireside Melodies

By the fire, we strum silly songs,
Making up lyrics, nothing feels wrong.
S'mores melt slow, gooey delight,
While the dog barks at the stars so bright.

Uncle Joe tunes his imaginary bass,
Laughter erupts, you can't keep pace.
Chairs are dancing, feet in the air,
It's a fireside party, the best kind of rare.

A Tapestry of Light

In the room, fairy lights twinkle and shine,
A carpet of giggles, just feel the design.
We weave silly stories, each thread a witticism,
Crafting a blanket of laughter's prism.

A tapestry woven from puns and plays,
Reminding us all of our brighter days.
With each stitch, we lift spirits so fine,
In this house of delight, everything's divine.

Under the Starry Veil

Beneath the sky, a dancing flea,
He whispered dreams to a lazy bee.
The stars were laughing, oh what a sight,
As the moon slipped in for a late-night bite.

A comet zoomed with a wondrous flair,
Chasing shooting stars, without a care.
The grasshoppers sang in a silly chime,
While a snail raced past — but took his time.

A squirrel did cartwheels, just for show,
While owls debated, 'How much wood can a crow throw?'
The night was young, full of giggly fun,
Under the veil, the laughter never done.

With every twinkle, a joke was shared,
The universe grinned, it truly cared.
So let's toast to the breezy tales spun,
Under the stars, we're all truly one.

Songs of Solace

In the kitchen, pots clanged like drums,
A cat's serenade, oh how it hums.
The fridge sang low, a tune so sweet,
Even the toaster joined in with a beat.

Oh, how the pancakes flip and fly,
While syrup drizzles like a sticky sky.
The coffee pot bubbled a boisterous tune,
As the sugar danced around like a loon.

The blender whirred, a zany machine,
Creating smoothies in colors unseen.
And as the toast popped up, it gave a cheer,
For breakfast parties are the best of the year.

In this kitchen dream, every bite is gold,
Each nibble brings laughter, tales retold.
We feast with joy until the sun goes down,
In our melody of meals, no room for a frown.

Where the Warmth Welcomes

In a cozy nook where shadows play,
The socks are mismatched, come what may.
A warm cup of tea, a comfy chair,
With a furry friend who doesn't care.

The fireplace crackles with joy and light,
As marshmallows roast, a gooey delight.
Cozy blankets piled high in a heap,
In this little den, we snooze and we leap.

The cat claims the best spot, as always found,
While we watch the flames dance round and round.
The chair creaks softly with secrets it knows,
As the laughter grows, like a garden that grows.

So here's to the warmth, where hearts intertwine,
In each goofy moment, like aged finest wine.
In spaces so snug, happiness blooms,
Where every corner welcomes, dispelling all glooms.

Heartstrings in the Hearth's Glow

When evening settles, the strings we strum,
A rabbit hops by — it's become quite numb.
The guitar's tuned to a silly song,
While we all laugh, as we sing along.

The candles flicker, with flames that dance,
While the dog attempts a bizarre prance.
Every note we play, a chuckle unfolds,
As stories of old get retold and retold.

The soup is bubbling, a funny smell,
With flavors mixed like a charming spell.
The whisk, it twirls like a ballerina,
While dinner's prep becomes a wild scene-a.

In the glow of the hearth, friendship grows bright,
With every strummed chord, our spirits take flight.
So here's to the laughter, the melodies flow,
In the heartstrings' embrace, we always glow.

Frost-Kissed Serenades

Snowflakes dance on my nose,
My cat thinks they're foes.
He pounces, he slips,
In the winter he trips.

Hot cocoa spills from my cup,
While marshmallows cheer, "Fill us up!"
But chocolate's a sneaky delight,
It hops in my mouth—what a sight!

My scarf's tangled around my face,
I can't see, I'm in a race.
But falling's my secret skill,
As I tumble down the hill.

Frost-kissed serenades do play,
Laughter echoes in a chilly way.
With snowman friends, we sing with glee,
Winter's a stage for you and me.

Emberlit Dreams

In the glow of evening's fire,
My socks tried to retire.
One jumped a little too high,
Now it sings in the sky!

Popcorn pops like jumping beans,
A buttery mess on my jeans.
The movie starts, but first,
I'll fix this popcorn burst.

S'mores are plans of sticky dreams,
Chocolate rivers, gooey streams.
But watch out for the marshmallow's flight,
It stuck to my hair last night!

Emberlit dreams keep me warm,
With laughter and smiles—a charm.
As the embers dance in delight,
It's the quirks that make life bright.

A Chorus of Frosted Whispers

Frosted whispers in the air,
My nose is blue, but who would care?
A snowball fight breaks out in glee,
But I'm hit! It was not meant for me!

Sledding down with a woosh and a bang,
My brother flew off—he really sang!
A sea of snow turns into a wave,
Funny memories are what we save.

The hot tub bubbles, we hop in wet,
A brave polar bear is what I bet.
But I can't find my warm sock's mate,
Is it hiding in the fridge? How great!

A chorus of laughter ignites the chill,
Chasing snowmen, we never stand still.
With winter's magic, we are in tune,
Singing joy to the snowy moon.

The Light of Togetherness

In the middle of the night,
We gather, sharing delight.
Cold feet dance on the floor,
While dad snores, we want more!

Candles flicker, shades of fun,
But my cat thinks they're on the run.
He leaps and knocks them right over,
In this chaos, we feel like a rover.

Games of charades, oh what a sight,
Grandma thinks she's a knight!
With raucous laughter, it can't be beat,
Who knew she can't handle defeat?

The light of togetherness shines bright,
Through giggles and sighs, it feels just right.
In every moment, our hearts align,
Creating memories, oh how divine!

Echoes of Frost and Fire

The flames they dance, a fiery show,
While frost tries hard to steal the glow.
A snowflake slips, it starts to slide,
Into the warmth, it tries to hide.

Yet ice can't crack a good old pun,
And fire just wants to have some fun.
Together they laugh, a witty pair,
Who knew a winter chill could share?

The embers glow, the frost does hiss,
It's quite a cozy, warmish bliss.
With jokes that burn and puns that freeze,
They light up nights with charming ease.

So here's to cold with jokes so bright,
And to the warmth that feels just right.
When frosty nights meet fiery flair,
Life's just a riot, if you dare!

Sips of Cheer and Melodic Whispers

A cup of cheer, let's take a sip,
While melodies dance, take a trip.
Rooftops hum with laughter light,
Underneath the stars so bright.

The tea is hot, the jokes are cold,
Stories exchanged, all anecdotes told.
With every sip, a smile blooms,
As laughter fills the cheery rooms.

Whispers float like gentle dreams,
Stirring up our happy schemes.
The good old songs drift through the air,
Mixing with giggles everywhere.

So raise your cups and toast to fun,
In friendship's warmth, we've surely won.
Sips of cheer and whispers sweet,
This vibrant life can't be beat!

The Stillness of a Singing Night

Under starry skies so bright,
The stillness hums, a singing night.
Crickets chirp their little tunes,
As moonlight dances with the dunes.

A stillness falls, a pause in air,
Yet laughter echoes everywhere.
With ghostly jokes that drift like mist,
Who knew the dark could be so blissed?

A songbird fluffs its feathery coat,
Sings lullabies on dreamy float.
Beneath the calm, the mischief swells,
With secrets whispered, silly spells.

So let the night wrap up tight,
In blankets sewn with pure delight.
When stillness sings, and giggles rise,
Magic glimmers in the skies!

Cradled in Warmth and Melody

In cozy nooks, we find our place,
With hot cocoa and smiles on face.
The melody sways through the room,
Chasing away all hints of gloom.

The laughter bubbles like a stream,
Together we weave the sweetest dream.
As marshmallows float, and giggles flare,
In cozy warmth, we haven't a care.

With every note that shimmers bright,
We cradle joy through the night.
Chasing shadows, we dance and sway,
In rhythm with warmth, we laugh and play.

So here's to the nights both soft and sweet,
Where warmth and melody are our treat.
In the heart's embrace, we twirl and spin,
Life reminds us, the joy's within!

Embers and Echoes of Togetherness

In the firelight's dance, we snicker,
S'mores are stuck, what a sticker!
With laughter warm, our hearts ignite,
Chasing shadows, as day turns night.

Hot cocoa spills, oh what a mess,
A marshmallow fight, who can guess?
We bundle close, a squishy herd,
With every joke, laughter's heard.

In the flicker, our secrets bloom,
Whispers shared in a cozy room.
When the moon dips low with a grin,
Together, we always win.

So here's to nights of warmth and fun,
With friends who shine brighter than the sun.
In every ember, a tale unfolds,
Echoes of joy, our bond retold.

The Gift of Song in Winter's Embrace

Snowflakes fall, a whimsical show,
We sing out loud, our voices flow.
A carol here, a jingle there,
Freezing notes fill the crisp, cool air.

With every note, our toes turn blue,
But the warmth inside feels oh so true!
Frosty fingers strumming away,
Musical mischief brightening the gray.

We hum a tune, the cat joins in,
A serenade to our frozen kin.
Winter's chill can't freeze our cheer,
In the gift of song, love is near.

Mismatched socks and off-key rhymes,
Laughing 'til we lose all times.
For in the winter's chilly grasp,
Together, we sing, together, we clasp.

Embers in the Glow

The embers flicker, what a sight!
Ghost stories told late at night.
Marshmallows roast, then down they go,
Caught in the fire's tantalizing glow.

We swap our tales of ghostly fright,
While whiskey warms with every bite.
The crackling wood, a soothing sound,
In this cozy circle, love is found.

Our laughter sparkles, like the flame,
No two stories are ever the same.
With every chuckle, embers soar,
Creating bonds that we adore.

So come gather 'round, share a cheer,
With friends like these, there's nothing to fear!
In the glow of warmth and light,
We'll forever stay close, day and night.

Melodies of Frost

The winter wind plays a tune so soft,
As snowflakes dance, they twirl aloft.
In hats and gloves, we twiddle away,
Creating melodies in a frosty play.

A snowman stands with a carrot nose,
But he can't sing, not even a prose!
Underneath the chilly azure sky,
We belt out notes and give it a try.

With slippery boots, we glide and sway,
Spreading joy in a wobbly way.
Each chuckle a note, each fall a beat,
In the symphony of cold, we find our heat.

So gather 'round for a fest of cheer,
For every melody, we hold dear.
In the frost, our spirits remain,
With laughter and song, we'll never wane.

Songs Wrapped in Warmth

In a cozy nook with tea, so fine,
Sipping slowly, feeling divine.
The cat sings loud, off-key but spry,
As the clock ticks by, oh my, oh my!

Cookie crumbs dance on my shirt,
While I ponder life over dessert.
The couch is plush, the TV's loud,
A ceremony of laziness—I'm proud!

Popsicle sticks for a masterpiece,
But my dog snatched it—what a tease!
I chase him 'round the living room,
Laughing loud, cloaked in my doom!

Oops, spilled coffee on my plans,
Guess that's how it goes with big hands.
Still wrapped in warmth, I'll take it slow,
Embracing chaos—the best show!

Nurtured Notes of Nature

In the garden where the daisies play,
A squirrel takes my sandwich away.
The bees buzz in a busy choir,
While I get chased by a plump old tire.

Dead leaves tumble with a squeaky sound,
As acorns fall upon the ground.
Birds sing tunes I can't quite catch,
While I dance awkwardly—a one-man match!

The sun shines bright; I start to bake,
Becoming one with the Earth, for pity's sake.
A ladybug lands on my nose,
I sneeze and watch it take to propose!

Nature's music, loud and clear,
Has me grinning from ear to ear.
But watch out for mud; it's a sly game,
One wrong step, and I'm a wet frame!

Celestial Gatherings

Under starry skies, the snacks are spread,
But I forgot the chips—it's a dread!
Aliens hover, asking for taste,
I offer them pickles, they flee in haste!

My telescope's a DIY from a can,
I intended stargazing, but there's a tan.
Constellations twinkle, oh what a sight,
But I can't find Orion—where's his light?

The moon takes selfies; it's quite the scene,
I wave back, hoping to look lean.
Flashes of laughter fill the cool air,
But my dance moves? A family affair!

Comets zoom by; we shout with glee,
But I just tripped over Auntie Lee.
In celestial gatherings, we chase the night,
With giggles and snacks—it feels so right!

An Evening of Togetherness

The table's set with mismatched plates,
Where everyone gathers—oh, what fun fates!
Uncle Joe spills wine on Grandma's dress,
We laugh it off; such a glorious mess!

The conversations swirl like the soup,
As cousins swap tales, creating a loop.
The jokes get louder, the punchlines hit,
And the dog decides it's time for a bit!

A game of charades erupts with zest,
But Aunt Sue's acting? Finding it's best!
With silly faces, and lots of cheer,
We cherish this moment, year after year.

As the night concludes and hugs are shared,
We know in our hearts, we truly cared.
An evening together, love fills the air,
With endless laughter, and dreams we dare!

Serenade of Starry Skies

The stars above, they wink and glow,
A cosmic show, a light-up disco.
Jupiter dances, Venus plays bass,
While Mars just sits, a grumpy face.

Comets streak across the night,
Like cats who've spotted something bright.
They zoom and zoom, then fade away,
Leaving us longing for another display.

In this celestial choir, we sing,
With galaxies swirling, joy's the thing.
So grab your blanket, lie back, recline,
In this starry ballet, we all align.

Oh, what a sight, this spacey spree,
Even black holes can't suck away our glee.
The universe laughs, and we join in,
With every twinkle, we simply grin.

Blended Voices beneath the Stars

Under the night, our voices blend,
Singing silly tunes that never end.
We croon about cats that dance and prance,
While tripping over feet in a cosmic trance.

The moon becomes our karaoke star,
As we belt out songs from here to afar.
The neighbors frown, but we just cheer,
In our moonlit choir, there's nothing to fear!

With each note, a mishap ensues,
As someone steps on toes and loses a shoe.
But laughter echoes, it's quite the scene,
Beneath the stars, we're a silly machine.

So join the chorus, let's raise our voice,
Tonight we make the universe rejoice.
Under starlit skies, we'll sing out loud,
Our blended voices, forever proud.

Songs of Hearth and Home

In the kitchen, pots go clang,
Mom's loud singing, it sure does hang.
Sizzling veggies and cookies galore,
Dance with aromas that we adore.

Dad's strumming softly, off-key delight,
While the dog joins in, barking with might.
We're a symphony of chaos, it's true,
In our cozy home, where love brews new.

Grandma's stories weave magic so fine,
About a potato that once was a swine.
With every tale, her laughter's in bloom,
While Grandpa just snores, lost in his room.

Family gatherings, the best kind of show,
With love, laughter, and more to bestow.
We'll cherish these songs, each quirky line,
In our heart's hearth, we all intertwine.

Illuminated Gatherings

Light up the night with our wild friends,
As lanterns bob and the music blends.
S'mores are melting, fire cracks and pops,
While everyone's taking hilarious flops.

With glow sticks twirling, we make a scene,
Dancing clumsily, all caught on film.
The night sky brightens with laughter and cheer,
As flashlights flicker, and everyone's near.

Tales of the past fly around the fire,
Each one's a gem that never gets tired.
We poke fun gently, no room for shame,
In our illuminated gathering – it's all just a game!

So here's to the moments that make us glow,
To the friends and the memories we love to stow.
When we're all together, nothing feels wrong,
In this merry chaos, we all belong.

Whispers of the Season

Leaves are falling, what a sight,
Dancing gently in delight.
Squirrels hoard their winter stash,
While I dream of pumpkin hash.

Sweaters come with arms so wide,
My coffee's hot, my friends, my pride.
Jumping in the leaf-mound bliss,
Oh, how I love autumn's kiss!

Crisp apples crunch as we all bite,
Yet I can't share, they're just too slight.
Hayrides bump along the way,
As farmers nod, they'll save the day.

So let us cheer with cider cups,
With friends around, who need more ups?
Laughter rings through every scene,
In whispered joy, we live the dream.

Threading Through Twilight

In twilight's grip, the day retreats,
With crickets chirping little beats.
The stars come out, they shine and wink,
While I roam close to the brink.

With shadows stretching, I must tread,
On paths where I might fear to tread.
But then I trip, my grace, unkind,
Who knew my foot would be that blind?

A ghostly fog rolls in with flair,
I question if it's hiding there.
"Hello?" I call, but silence reigns,
Just me and my embarrassing claims.

Yet as I stumble, laugh I must,
For evening strolls are made of dust.
With every step, a tale is spun,
Of misadventures, oh what fun!

The Fire's Caress

The flames are dancing, oh so bright,
They take the chill right out of night.
I roast my marshmallow with care,
But my stick is missing, I despair!

The sparks fly high, like little stars,
While I avoid my friend's guitar.
With each strum, they laugh and shout,
It's all in jest, or so they tout!

I drop my s'more into the sand,
The sumptuous treat slips from my hand.
My friends all laugh, they can't believe,
How clumsy I am, oh, what a reprieve!

Yet in this warmth, we share our tales,
Of summer nights and past travails.
Together round the fire's cheer,
We find our joy and hold it near.

Hushed Echoes of the Heart

A whisper floats, so soft, so sweet,
It tickles gently at my feet.
Romance blooms in awkward ways,
Like texting late on dreary days.

The heart does dance, though late it sings,
Caught in webs of silly things.
I seek your eyes in crowded rooms,
Yet trip on carpets, that's my doom!

Your laughter rings, a bright refrain,
Yet I just blush, oh what a pain!
In every chance, I take a shot,
My brave facade, though feels so not.

But in these echoes, hope's alive,
In every word, we choose to strive.
With whispered dreams and silly parts,
We paint the canvas of our hearts.

Hearthside Whispers

In front of the fire, there's a cat on my lap,
She dreams of a feast, a tuna fish snack.
The flames dance and flicker, it's cozy and bright,
While I'm stuck with leftovers, it's quite the plight.

The stockings are hung with care on the wall,
But Santa might trip, and that'd be a fall!
I leave him some cookies, he eats them all quick,
Guess he's too busy, he won't hear my sick trick!

Grandma's tall tales, they never grow old,
About the time she wrestled a bear, so bold.
With eggnog in hand, we giggle and cheer,
Just don't ask her that story again next year!

The dog steals the biscuits, he's quick on his feet,
While cousins debate if fruitcake's a treat.
We laugh and we joke by the warm, crackling light,
Hearthside whispers keep us cozy tonight.

Carols by Candlelight

Oh, deck the halls with boughs of folly,
Uncle Jim sings loud, we all start to lolly.
He thinks he's the star, but wait 'til we see,
Grandma's sharp notes are a pitch off-key!

The kids run around, all hopped up on sweets,
While Edwin thinks he can dance on his feet.
He twirls with the cat, what a sight to behold,
Hope the cat knows karate, or it'll end up rolled!

We hum along softly, but then hear a crash,
Looks like Aunt Sue's got a thing for the stash.
She's off-key for sure, but in holiday cheer,
We know she's the reason we laugh so sincere!

So here's to the carols, both joyful and jolly,
As we sing through the night, what a merry folly!
With candles aglow, and the laughter we bring,
In this charming chaos, our hearts brightly sing!

Yule Log Serenade

Gather 'round folks, the log's on the fire,
We'll sing to the flames, it's our heart's desire.
But Dad's lost a marshmallow, now it's stuck on the roof,

Not for the first time, that's a well-known goof!

The kids make a wish as they toss in the wood,
While Mom rolls her eyes, 'If it only could!'
The smoke starts to choke us, what a fragrant delight,
Is it the s'mores or Uncle Bob's socks? Quite a fright!

As we roast our chestnuts, they jump and they pop,
I swear that one flipped, and oh, there it went plop!
While laughter surrounds, it dances on air,
Who knew holiday woes could be filled with such flair?

So here's to the Yule log, and the memories made,
Of laughter and stories that never do fade.
With each flip of the marshmallow, another cheer might arise,
'Cause family and fun bring us the greatest surprise!

Soft Shadows and Sweet Echoes

In the soft glow of night, with shadows that play,
The carolers come, what a quirky display!
They sing like old frogs, but with all of their might,
Might even wake neighbors for a hello goodnight!

The cookies go missing; who's this sneaky thief?
Looks like Timmy's taken his holiday grief.
He grins with crumbs stuck all over his face,
We're still all just happy, there's laughter in space!

The lights on the tree twinkle bright in delight,
While Dad finds the tinsel, stuck in his sight.
He thinks he's a pro, but alas, it's a mess,
We all stand and chuckle, he's decked in distress!

With sweet echoes of joy filling warmth in our hearts,
This holiday season just never departs.
We craft our own magic, in soft shadow's play,
Creating each moment, in our funny old way!

A Tapestry of Warmth

In a quilt made of laughter, all colors collide,
A spoon in my hand, I'm ready to bide.
With pie crumbs a-flying, and joy in the air,
I'm knitting my dreams without a care.

A stitch of good feelings, with threads of delight,
Each knot is a giggle, each patch is a sight.
Bring on the warmth, it's time for a feast,
Who knew that grandmas could be such a beast?

The cats are all fighting for my cozy chair,
While I juggle the snacks like I haven't a care.
With ice cream for breakfast and toast on a shoe,
Contemplating life with a wacky crew.

So let's wrap up in laughter, stitch tightly with cheer,
In this tapestry woven, there's nothing to fear.
For warmth is more than a cozy embrace,
It's the joy in the faces we love in this place.

Chorus of Kindness

In a land made of smiles, where kindness is king,
A parrot sings songs of the joy that we bring.
With hugs like a blanket, and winks like a game,
It's a chorus of kindness, and nothing's the same.

The giraffes join the dance, with their necks swaying high,

While penguins do the cha-cha, oh me, oh my!
Squirrels in tuxedos offer nuts on a plate,
With a bow and a shimmy, they're never late.

A cat with a bow tie recites lovely prose,
While the dogs bark along, with a tune that just flows.
Kindness is catchy, it spreads like a cheer,
In this odd little concert, you've nothing to fear.

So come grab a partner, let's dance 'til we drop,
In this chorus of kindness, we'll never quite stop.
With jokes and with laughter, we'll brighten the day,
In the land full of kindness, that's where we will play.

Evening Ember Echoes

As the sun starts to dip, with a sizzle and pop,
The fireflies flicker, as shadows will hop.
In the glow of the evening, the crickets do sing,
With marshmallows roasting, oh what joy they bring!

The stars start to twinkle, with mischief in sight,
While we toast to the moon that just framed the night.
With giggles that echo, we share all our charms,
Wrapped up by the fire, in warmth of our arms.

A raccoon in a hat thinks he's part of the show,
He juggles our leftover s'mores, don't you know?
With laughter and stories, our spirits will soar,
In the evening's embrace, we're never a bore!

So here's to the darkness, where laughter ignites,
In the glow of the embers, we'll dream all our sights.
With joy in the echoes that night-time can lend,
May the magic of evening never come to an end.

Flickers of Joy

A pancake flipped high, it lands with a thud,
The syrup's a river, the butter's a flood.
In the kitchen, the chaos is a marvelous sight,
With flour in my hair, I'm a baker tonight!

A dance down the hallway, I trip on my shoe,
Each wobble and giggle just adds to the view.
With socks on the floor and a cat on my feet,
This mess is a treasure, it's joy on repeat!

The sunbeams are tickling my toes on the ground,
As I twirl like a dervish, all feeling unbound.
With chuckles a-plenty and snacks piled up high,
I'm a flicker of joy, I'm ready to fly!

So grab all your dreams, let's dance through the air,
For joy is the spark, the giggle we share.
With a sprinkle of laughter and a dash of delight,
We'll flicker and twinkle, like stars in the night.

Embers of Togetherness

In the kitchen, a pot's on the boil,
A lid that's too tight, a chef's sure to toil.
We laugh as the noodles take flight,
And spaghetti's now a ceiling's delight.

The cat steals a piece, with sneaky grace,
While the dog looks on with a puzzled face.
We all share a joke, a pun that ignites,
As warmth fills the room on chilly nights.

Grandma's stories twinkle like stars,
While Uncle Bob claims he once drove a car.
These tales, though strange, help us unite,
In the embers of laughter, we find our light.

So here's to the chaos, the mess and the cheer,
To cooking disasters that bring us near.
Together we bumble, together we shine,
In this funny dance of intertwining time.

Caroling Beneath the Ember Sky

We gather 'round, with songs in our hearts,
Bundled in layers, oh, winter imparts.
The snowflakes fall with a giggly sound,
While off-key carolers are proudly found.

A cat in a scarf joins the festive show,
With a meow that signals, 'It's time to go!'
We belt out tunes, the neighbors complain,
But joy's in the air, so who has the gain?

Hot cocoa spills, and marshmallows fly,
As we slip on the ice, with a gleeful sigh.
The stars overhead, like glitter, they glow,
Beneath the ember sky, our spirits flow.

With laughter and joy, we dance in the night,
Each note a reminder, everything's right.
In this quirky life, full of weather and cheer,
We carol together, year after year.

The Sweet Aroma of Joyful Gatherings

The oven buzzes, a cake on the rise,
But Dad's got his secrets, like a master of pies.
Mom adds some sprinkles with a flick and a whiff,
While Auntie brings cookies, all sweet with a tiff.

The table's a canvas of flavors and cheer,
With dishes aplenty from far and near.
We toast with our glasses of soda so bright,
As laughter erupts, oh, what a sight!

We share funny stories with flavors to match,
Like the time Cousin Dave tried to fix the old hatch.
A burst of laughter as we tell that tale,
His soup was a rocket that sadly set sail.

Through crumbs on our shirts and spills on the ground,
We savor each moment, the joy that we've found.
With each tasty bite and every loud cheer,
The sweet aroma of love lingers near.

Silhouettes in the Radiant Light

As evening falls, we gather once more,
With candles flickering, laughter to score.
In the radiant glow, our shadows take flight,
Dancing and twirling, a hilarious sight.

The stories get bolder, as shadows grow tall,
While someone trips over a blanket, oh no!
With a laugh and a grin, they rise to their feet,
Claiming it was part of the dance, oh so neat.

Outside, the moon beams a curious gaze,
While we bumble about in our jovial phase.
Silhouette silliness, all piled in one room,
With giggles and glares that lighten the gloom.

So here's to the moments, both silly and sweet,
In the glow of the night, where our laughter's the beat.
In the warmth of togetherness, we find our might,
As silhouettes dance in the radiant light.

A Tapestry of Christmas Serenades

Oh jingle bells, how they ring,
A cat on the tree, what a thing!
Mom's fruitcake, a family plight,
Gingerbread men ready for flight.

Socks hung with care, near the flame,
One of them's missing, whose game?
Wrap the gifts in paper, so bright,
Tape stuck to my fingers, oh right!

Carols sung out of tune, what a show,
Santa's lost GPS, where did he go?
Rudolph's red nose is now green,
What a sight, the strangest you've seen!

As we gather for dinner, what fun,
Uncle Bob's stories, he's always the one.
The roast is burnt, but who really cares?
We'll feast on leftovers, if anyone dares!

Flickering Lights and Gentle Songs

The lights on the tree, just a mess,
A squirrel got in, what a stress!
Twinkling bright, yet still askew,
Is that a garland or spaghetti too?

Snowflakes fall, not one is the same,
But my snowman looks rather lame.
His arms are twigs, one fell off,
'Tis the season to laugh and scoff!

Eggnog spills, a slippery floor,
Dad's dancing like he's done it before.
The carols echo, voices off-key,
Yet we sing along joyfully!

So gather round, let's share a cheer,
With laughter and joy, we hold dear.
For in our hearts, this truth remains,
It's the silly times that bring the gains!

Hearthside Tales in the Snow

By the fire, hot cocoa in hand,
Tales of snowmen that couldn't stand.
A snowball fight that lasted too long,
Next year we'll write a fairer song.

The dog in a sweater, oh the delight,
Chasing snowflakes, what a funny sight!
Mom's sock monkey hangs from the tree,
Its eyes are staring back at me!

Frosty's nose a carrot, but not a clue,
It's actually from the fridge, who knew?
The snow is thick, and so's the fun,
We'll build a new friend, or just run!

As winter nights stretch, the stories unfold,
Of elves and reindeer, and goodies untold.
We laugh and recall each silly blunder,
Finding joy in the magic of wonder!

Echoes of Laughter and Light

In the crisp air, giggles abound,
The snowman is melting, can we save him, profound?
With carrots and buttons, we tried our best,
But he's won the award for the funniest guest!

Cookies are baking, a floury fight,
Mom's powdered wig looks like a sight.
The oven's too hot, oh what a mess,
But who can resist this holiday stress?

Sledding downhill, oh what a speed,
Crash into snowdrifts, now that's quite a deed!
With cheeks all aglow from the wintery chill,
These memories created give us a thrill.

So let's raise a glass, toast and say,
To laughter and light, on this fine day!
In the chaos, we find simple cheer,
Together we shine, all through the year!

Gentle Breaths of December

The snowflakes dance like paper swans,
As reindeer sweep the lawn with brawn.
Hot chocolate spills and marshmallows fly,
While the cat plots mischief, oh so sly.

Jingle bells ring from a rusty old bike,
An elf forgot his hat, what a hike!
Grandma's cookies, a secret delight,
They vanish quicker than a star at night.

Icicles hang like chandeliers grand,
And snowmen wave with a frozen hand.
Winter's a party, though cold, it seems,
We laugh at the snow, but crave summer dreams.

Stringed Harmonies by the Fire

The guitar strums out a silly tune,
While the cat serenades the full moon.
Fingers fumble, the chords go awry,
And Aunt Mabel sleeps with a satisfied sigh.

The marshmallows roast like stars in the sky,
While Uncle Bob tastes his own infamous pie.
With each awkward chord and a chuckle or two,
We know the night's magic comes from the crew.

The flames crackle like a witty old joke,
As shadows dance, and laughter awoke.
With each note played, the night hums along,
Even the chairs seem to sway in our song.

Captured in Warmth

Wrapped in blankets, we gather around,
In this cozy cocoon, all worries are drowned.
The dog steals the spot where we all once laid,
Snoring away like a furry parade.

The popcorn's a treasure, the movie's a flop,
But Grandma's narration makes our sides pop.
Every twist and turn brings a volley of glee,
As the popcorn lobbed bounces off me.

Laughter keeps bubbling like a warm winter stew,
With jests and its echoes, we both stick like glue.
Captured in warmth, we delight in the hour,
Finding joy in the silly, a whimsical power.

Glow of the Solstice Heart

The solstice glows with a warm, bright charm,
As the earth wraps up its wintery harm.
We dance with socks that don't quite match,
And pretend that we're stars in a cosmic patch.

The lights twinkle like fireflies in a jar,
While the dog finds cheer in a rubbery star.
With eggnog mustaches, we raise a loud cheer,
To all things absurd, to those we hold dear.

With each happy moment, we laugh and we sing,
Enjoying the chaos the holiday brings.
In the glow of togetherness, hearts truly shine,
Like the golden lights draping the old pine.

The Glow of Community

In the park, we gather round,
Swapping tales, laughter sound.
Bring your snacks, no need for grace,
Last week's leftovers? What a taste!

Neighbors bicker, who's to blame?
Was it Gary or was it Jane?
Kids are running with sticky hands,
Who knew friendship comes with bands?

Old Mr. Frank shows off his skills,
Balances pies and gives us thrills.
We clap and cheer, can't believe our eyes,
He's the star under these sunny skies!

Each smile shared lights up the night,
In our little town, everything's right.
So join the fun, don't be a bore,
Our community needs you – the fun's in store!

Nights Wrapped in Light

Stars are shining, what a show,
But don't ask me, I'm a no-go.
I tripped and fell on my own shoe,
Now I'm just lying here like goo!

Campfire crackles, we roast s'mores,
But watch out, my friend – it roars!
Smoke alarms shout, we all disperse,
Is that a blessing, or just worse?

The night is bright, but I can't see,
My marshmallow just ate me!
Let's light up the night with laughter loud,
No wonder we're all so proud!

When daylight comes, we'll tell the tale,
Of how our night sparked a big fail.
Yet deep inside, we know it's right,
To laugh and love on this starry night!

Cherished Moments by the Hearth

Gather 'round, it's time to feast,
But Aunt Mildred's jokes just won't cease.
"Why did the chicken cross the floor?"
To avoid the jokes that we all bore!

Soup is bubbling, warm and bright,
But what's that smell? It's not quite right!
"Did someone burn the garlic bread?"
Oh dear, I think we're all misled.

Grandpa snores in his comfy chair,
While we take selfies, unaware.
"Say cheese!" I shout, but he just snores,
The funniest picture, he brings high scores!

Yet these moments, even if askew,
Are cherished and dear, me and you.
With laughter and warmth, our hearts are tied,
By the fireside, love is our guide!

Winter's Chorus of Harmony

Snowflakes falling, a ballet so fine,
But wait—what's that? Is it a sign?
Bob's stuck in the snow, waving his arms,
Help him out, with his winter charms!

Sledding thrills and laughter explode,
Down the hill, we take the code.
But oh dear, I've lost my sled,
Now I'm rolling, that's how I spread!

Hot cocoa warming in everyone's hands,
But who put marshmallows all in our bands?
A sweet surprise, or a gooey mess,
Winter gatherings, we must confess!

Through all the snow and chilly breeze,
Our hearts are glowing, we share with ease.
In winter's grip, we find our cheer,
This chorus of joy, so bright and clear!

Echoes of the Night

The moon forgot to wear its shoes,
It stumbled over clouds to snooze.
The stars are giggling, what a sight,
As crickets sing with all their might.

A bat flew by, a blundering fright,
Who knew they could get such a height?
An owl hooted, 'Who's there tonight?'
The jokes and jests take playful flight.

Shadows dance and join the fun,
While raccoons plot their mischief run.
The night is full of silly schemes,
As laughter drifts in dreamlike beams.

Candlelit Chimes

The candles flicker with a grin,
They're gossiping where they've been.
The shadows laugh, they love to tease,
As wax drips down with little ease.

A tea set chats with silver spoons,
Discussing antics of the moons.
The curtains dance with merry glee,
In this delightfully dim spree.

The clock strikes twelve, it's time to bust,
A cha-cha line of cakes and crust.
With every ding, the laughter swells,
These candlelit friends are quite theells!

Savoring the Season's Glow

Pumpkin pie with a wink and sigh,
Whispers of spice that soar and fly.
Apple bobbing competitors frown,
If only the apples would stop going down!

Sweaters hug with cozy cheer,
One's got a stain, oh dear, oh dear!
Hot cocoa mustache, a sight to show,
With marshmallow smiles, steal the glow!

Leaves swirling like they'll break a rule,
While squirrels plot to take back their school.
Nature's painting, oh what a show,
In this fantastical, edible flow!

The Magic of Gathering

Friends come leaping through the door,
With all their quirks, how can you ignore?
One brings jokes that bounce and dive,
While another stirs the laughs alive.

Chairs are filled with giggles bright,
As stories twist into the night.
The punch bowl's bubbling like a witch,
Ensuring everyone's quite a pitch!

Games of charades bring silly faces,
As we tumble through crowded spaces.
The magic sparkles in our chest,
In gatherings, truly, we are blessed!

Warmth in the Whispering Pines

In the pines where squirrels dart,
A trombone croaks, a dog plays art.
The trees gossip, bark and sway,
They really have too much to say.

Pinecones drop with comedic flair,
Kidding the boots that are laid bare.
The sunlight glints, the shadows tease,
A raccoon hums, "Please share the cheese!"

The breeze has jokes, it tickles me,
Leaves laugh out loud, oh what a spree!
A picnic planned, oh what a sight,
But the ants hold court; they bite and bite!

Nature's whimsy, so lighthearted,
Each laugh shared beats even the charted.
In whispering winds, we find our cheer,
Just watch out, they might steal your beer!

The Glow of Hearthside Harmony

By the hearth where warmth doth dance,
A cat takes charge, as if by chance.
Old socks become a pillow throne,
While marshmallows sing, "We're not alone!"

The fire crackles, pops with glee,
Pants on fire? No, just poetry!
The cocoa swirls, a chocolate whirl,
As shoes become a waltzing girl.

Uncles crack jokes, each one worse than last,
The kids roll eyes, it's all a blast.
The flames grow higher, sparks take flight,
Even the shadows giggle at night!

Gather round for tales absurd,
Every story needs a silly word.
In this glow, all troubles cease,
Who knew warmth could bring such peace?

Melodies of Winter's Embrace

Oh winter's chill gives way to cheer,
As snowflakes dance and twirl, oh dear!
The penguins slide down on their backs,
Snowmen have conversations, no lack!

Hot cider served with a side of laughs,
The snowball fight leads to silly gaffes.
A dog in boots, what a sight to see,
He plows through snow, as proud as can be!

Icicles dangling with a wink,
The kids all ponder—did they drink?
The stars above are twinkling bright,
While reindeer practice their Wednesday flight.

The season hums a frosty tune,
With every giggle beneath the moon.
So bundle up, let's join the cheer,
In winter's hug, we persevere!

Flickers and Chants of Yuletide

In December's chill, the lights go bright,
The trees wear hats, what a silly sight!
Elves shuffle around with candy canes,
While Santa's stuck in the window panes!

Cookies baked with zero defense,
Mice hold parties, it makes no sense.
As reindeer trot on rooftops high,
They'll steal your milk, oh my, oh my!

The carolers sing with voices cracked,
Ignoring the dog who's having a snack.
Jingle bells ring, though one's out of tune,
It's all just chaos beneath the moon!

So gather close, sing loud and free,
Remember laughter's the best recipe!
For Yuletide brings joy, mixed with delight,
And gifts of humor keep spirits bright!

The Dance of the Warmth

The sun rose high, what a sight,
The squirrels all squeaked in delight.
With ice cream cones in hand we cheer,
As winter's chill just disappears.

The beachball bounces, oh what fun,
Chasing it under the glaring sun.
A flip-flop flies, a dog gives chase,
I hope he finds that shoe, what a race!

We barbecue while the sun shines bright,
Grill smoke swirling, what a delight.
But watch for the bees, they're quite the crowd,
They love the sweet stuff, singing loud!

So let's dance and twirl in the warm day,
Laughing together, come what may.
With warmth all around, we've nothing to fear,
Except maybe a sunburn, oh dear!

Whims of Winter Night

The snowflakes dance in the moon's glow,
An igloo stands proudly, not too slow.
Snowmen rock hats and big carrot noses,
While children throw snowballs, just like roses.

A polar bear slips on a slick ice patch,
It's quite the scene, a perfect mismatch.
The owls are hooting quite late at night,
While reindeer work hard to get in flight.

Hot cocoa flows, with marshmallows piled,
We sip and we giggle, like a bunch of wild.
The frost on the windows tells stories of fun,
As we snuggle together, our hearts become one.

What a wintery whimsy, let it last long,
In our flannel pajamas, we all sing a song.
With laughter and joy, we'll take our sweet time,
In this whimsical night, all's perfectly prime!

Charm of the Cheerful

A smile so wide, it lights the road,
Bringing sunshine wherever one strode.
With jokes and riddles, no frowns in sight,
It's a charm to be cheerful, oh what delight!

With googly eyes on muffins displayed,
And a wiggle dance, we're all dismayed!
The fish in the tank do a funny jig,
As laughter erupts, it grows big and big.

The sun beams down on all of our games,
While we act like goofballs, adding new names.
A silly hat on a cat makes us grin,
Laughter and merriment where we fit in.

So hold your smiles, wear your best cheer,
In this charming life, we've nothing to fear.
With friends all around, let's sing and let's play,
Let's spread some joy, come what may!

A Canvas of Kindness

Brushes dancing on colors so bright,
Each stroke of kindness, a marvelous sight.
On this canvas, let's paint with love,
Like a dove, flying free up above.

A splash of joy on a gloomy day,
Sprinkling cheer in a friendly way.
The more we share, the more it grows,
Like a garden of kindness, everybody knows.

With each little act, we paint a new hue,
A rolling laughter, like morning dew.
A smile gifted here, a hug over there,
Turns our canvas into a masterpiece rare.

So let us create, with laughter and cheer,
A beautiful world, we hold so dear.
With brushes of kindness, we'll paint the sky,
In this lovely canvas, together we fly!

Hearth-bound Wordsmiths

In the glow of the firelight's dance,
Writers ponder their next advance.
With coffee cups and snacks galore,
They scribble tales of folklore.

A cat jumps up, spills tea with flair,
They gasp, hands flying through the air.
"A plot twist lost!" a writer cries,
While their muse just rolls its eyes.

With laughter loud, they share a pun,
"Why did the writer skip the run?
Too much plot, not enough pace,
But look! I've won the coffee race!"

So here's a toast, let's mix and blend,
To hearth-bound friends, a joyful trend.
With quills in hand and hearts so bold,
They write their stories, pure as gold.

Serenades of the Season

In springtime blooms, a sneezing fit,
The flowers shout, "We're a perfect hit!"
While bees go buzzing, seeking treats,
Allergies dance on happy feet.

Come summer's heat, the ice cream melts,
As kids on bikes do summer belts.
They tumble, giggle, fall and cheer,
"My cone's a hat, look what I wear!"

Then autumn leaves, a crinkle sound,
The squirrels scurry, nuts abound.
With every crunch, their secrets told,
"Winter's coming, let's all be bold!"

And winter comes with frosty cheer,
"Who made me wear this snowman gear?"
But hot cocoa keeps spirits bright,
Serenades of season's delight!

The Warmth of Community Spirit

In the park, a potluck spread,
Baked beans and laughter, good times ahead.
Grandma's pie, a legendary feat,
It won't last long with all this heat.

A dog runs by, wearing a cape,
"Super Pup!" we all escape.
With frisbees flying, and kids in tow,
Community spirit, we all glow.

The fire pit roars, stories ignite,
"Remember when?" under the night.
Neighbors share tales of failure,
"I'm still recovering from that 'baker'!"

So let's raise a glass, cheers all around,
For laughter and love, in friendship found.
Together we thrive, under the sun,
In our cozy space, we are all one.

Flickering Shadows

By the campfire, shadows twist,
Ghost stories told, can't resist.
"But I swear, it was just a glare!"
"Yeah, right, you're just too scared to share!"

A stick snaps loud, a raccoon screams,
"Let's stick to s'mores and share our dreams!"
"Do raccoons plot? Are they in a band?"
"Oh, stop it now, they're just way too planned!"

Through the flicker, faces beam bright,
With chuckles and cheers, we own the night.
"But which way home? I think I'm lost!"
"Relax, my friend, at least we're not tossed."

So gather 'round the fiery glow,
In laughter's warmth, we surely grow.
As shadows dance, our spirits ignite,
In this funny chaos, all feels right.

Harmonious Hearts

In the choir, voices blend strong,
But one poor soul can't find the song.
"Is this the key?" they ask in dread,
While others sing; they just misled.

The conductor waves, arms like a bird,
"Let's harmonize!" almost absurd.
With giggles stuck behind each note,
A cat joins in—this harmony's wrote!

With ukuleles strumming, smiles are wide,
"Have you tried adding a pet as a guide?"
With cats and dogs helping the beat,
Music's a ruckus, can't handle defeat!

So raise your voice, let laughter ring,
In this chorus of joy, together we sing.
For in every heart, there's a silly part,
That makes us one with harmonies start.

Echoes of the Ember

The fire crackles, sparks take flight,
I thought I brought s'mores, but brought a bite!
My friend roasted marshmallows, started to giggle,
Until he burned his eyebrows, oh what a wiggle!

The shadows dance, making shapes on the grass,
I told a joke, but it didn't quite pass.
The crickets laughed, they chirped with delight,
As the flames started popping, we fled from the sight.

We roasted hot dogs, but they turned to ash,
Then tossed them to raccoons, who made quite the splash.

With laughter surrounding our late-night endeavor,
Who knew camping could be such a treasure?

But as the embers die down to a glow,
We'll hoot like an owl, put on a show.
Just remember the marshmallows, they never get old,
Unless they turn into a crispy, brown mold!

Twinkling Lights and Gentle Nights

In the dark, the stars play hide and seek,
I tripped on a rock, oh, what a squeak!
The moon winked down, said, 'Don't lose your way,'
I waved back politely, then started to sway.

The fireflies buzzed in a shimmering dance,
While I tried to woo one with my goofy prance.
They laughed and they flickered, said, 'Not tonight!'
So I settled for shadows, out of mind, out of sight.

At midnight a hoot, from an owl in a tree,
I asked for his wisdom, he just hooted with glee.
"Life's like the night, full of quirky delights,"
But I lost my shoe, cost me two laughs and fights.

But every twinkle, each glimmering spark,
Makes me chuckle there in the dark.
For in gentle nights, with giggles and fright,
We dance like the stars, oh, what a sight!

Serenading the Stillness

The stillness calls like a cat with a purr,
But I break the silence, causin' quite a stir!
My off-key voice, a serenade unique,
Even the crickets said, 'No thanks, we're bleak!'

The moon rolled his eyes, said, 'Do you hear that?'
Even the trees bent low, laughing at my chat.
I thought I was smooth, with a poetic twist,
But the nearby dogs just howled and hissed!

As I serenade shadows, they start to sway,
Mocking my rhythms in their own clever way.
An audience of bugs joins in with their zap,
While I trip over roots, into a damp lap.

But laughter's the tune that plays on repeat,
In this symphony of life, so strange but sweet.
So I carry on singing, off-pitch and in jest,
For serenading stillness is truly the best!

The Warmth of Kindred Voices

Gather 'round friends, with stories to share,
But one slips on soda and ends up in a chair!
We'll laugh 'til we cry, or just nearly fall,
With the warmth of kindred voices, we'll outshout it all.

In the glow of the fire, the jokes start to fly,
We recollect moments that make time sigh.
One friend's attempting to play on the flute,
But it sounds more like a distressed, squeaky boot!

As we swap silly tales that rhyme and entwine,
The warmth of the night feels so perfectly fine.
Our hearts create songs of love and of cheer,
And I promise, I'll not let you vanish, my dear!

So here's to the laughter, the friendship, the giggles,
With snacks piled high, it's a night that just wiggles.
Together we're stronger, in laughter we lift,
With the warmth of our voices, oh what a gift!

A Symphony of Warmth and Wonder

In socks that don't quite match our style,
We dance in circles, but not with guile.
The dog joins in, a pup with flair,
As we twirl and tumble without a care.

The fridge is full, the snacks are loud,
We feast like kings, feeling so proud.
But what's that smell? A mystery dear,
Just guacamole gone rogue, I fear!

The cat rolls over, giving us shade,
While we attempt our grand charade.
A symphony of laughter fills the air,
As we wave our arms, like we just don't care.

So let the warmth and wonder unfold,
With stories shared, and memories bold.
In this quirky chaos, we find delight,
A crazy family, oh what a sight!

Shadows Dancing in the Warm Glow

In our living room, the shadows play,
They twist and turn in a funny ballet.
My uncle's snoring, a bass in tune,
As the cat performs under the moon.

The light flickers on and off with glee,
Making monsters of my aunt with a cup of tea.
She jumps and yelps, we're all in stitches,
How shadows can cause such funny glitches!

The dog is confused, he chases his tail,
While the shadows dance, they never fail.
A wonderland formed in our cozy den,
A ballet of shadows, let's do it again!

So gather 'round with snacks in hand,
As shadows waltz to our laughter's band.
In the warm glow of the night's embrace,
We find pure joy in this silly space!

Songs Beneath a Starlit Canopy

Under stars so bright, we sing off-key,
The frogs join in, oh what harmony!
A campfire crackles, roasting marshmallows,
While my sister tries to serenade the swallows.

The guitar's out of tune, but who really cares?
We're swaying and laughing, trading our glares.
My brother insists he can catch a breeze,
But it's just the smoke that makes him sneeze!

The night sky twinkles with stories to tell,
Of a bear that danced, oh can you tell?
We keep the rhythm with our clumsy feet,
As we moonwalk to the sound of our beat.

So under this canopy, so rich and wide,
We find our joy, our voices collide.
With songs so silly and hearts full of cheer,
We'll serenade the stars, at least until we hear!

Whispers of Tradition and Love

In the kitchen's warmth, traditions collide,
Grandma's secret recipe she cannot hide.
With sauce stains on her favorite dress,
She stirs the pot, we're quite the mess.

A pinch of laughter, a splash of cheer,
While dad attempts to cook, and we all sneer.
The smoke alarms wail—a familiar sound,
As he brandishes spatulas, love all around.

We gather 'round the table, it's quite the scene,
Pass the burnt potatoes, never so keen.
Yet in these moments, we find a treasure,
Laughter and love, our sweetest measure.

So here's to the whispers of family lore,
In traditions that bind, we're always wanting more.
With every mishap and every cheer,
In the warmth of our home, we hold each dear.

Milton Keynes UK
Ingram Content Group UK Ltd.
UKHW010228111224
452348UK00011B/576